Language Builders

Cailyn and Chloe Learn about
CONJUNCTIONS

by Megan Atwood
illustrated by Estudio Haus

Content Consultant
Roxanne Owens
Associate Professor, Elementary Reading
DePaul University

NORWOODHOUSE PRESS
CHICAGO, ILLINOIS

Norwood House Press
P.O. Box 316598
Chicago, Illinois 60631
For information regarding Norwood House Press, please visit
our website at:
www.norwoodhousepress.com or call 866-565-2900.

Editor: Arnold Ringstad
Designer: Jake Nordby
Project Management: Red Line Editorial

Library of Congress Cataloging-in-Publication Data
Atwood, Megan, author.
  Cailyn and Chloe learn about conjunctions / by Megan Atwood
; illustrated by Estudio Haus.
     p. cm. -- (Language Builders)
  Includes bibliographical references.
  Summary: "Cailyn and Chloe use conjunctions as they write
an article about a neighborhood block party for their school
newspaper. Concepts include: basic definition and usage of
conjunctions; coordinating; correlative and subordinating
conjunctions. Activities in the back help reinforce text concepts.
Includes glossary and additional resources"-- Provided by
publisher.
  Audience: Ages 7-10
  ISBN 978-1-59953-671-2 (library edition : alk. paper) -- ISBN
978-1-60357-731-1 (ebook)
  1. English language--Conjunctions--Juvenile literature. 2.
English language--Grammar--Juvenile literature. I. Estudio Haus
(Firm) II. Title.
  PE1345.A89 2015
  428.1--dc22
                              2014030265

Manufactured in the United States of America in North
Mankato, Minnesota.
262N—122014

Words in **black bold** are defined in the glossary.

Talk about Connections!

Today in class Mr. Rosen taught us about **conjunctions**. We practiced writing sentences using them. He said conjunctions are all about connecting and combining things. That's something I love to do!

Then, Mr. Rosen also talked about writing for the school newspaper. I told my best friend, Chloe, that we could write an article using conjunctions! Chloe and I live near each other, and we know the perfect thing to report on: our neighborhood block party. Mr. Rosen says the writers of the best article will win a prize. Chloe and I are going to write the best story we can. We'll also try to use the three kinds of conjunctions we learned about in class. Wish us luck!

By Cailyn, age 10

"Chloe, it's starting!" Cailyn knocked hard on the door. Chloe soon opened it and gave a wide smile.

"I've got my notebook for our article," she said, waving it in front of Cailyn's face. Cailyn giggled. They had the exact same notebook.

Cailyn said, "They're setting up for the block party. We had better get going." The two girls walked down the street. They saw their neighbors setting everything up. Cailyn's parents, Mrs. and Mr. Conrad, put food on a long table. Chloe's mom, Mrs. Carlson, helped set up a volleyball net. Some younger kids were playing tag. Just then, Chloe spotted something amazing.

"Cailyn, look!" Chloe said. "They even have a bouncy castle!" The two friends grinned at each other.

But then Cailyn's face got serious. "Okay, we need to start the newspaper article for our school assignment. Remember, Mr. Rosen said to use as many conjunctions as we can in the article."

Chloe nodded. "I can't remember all three types—can you?"

Cailyn said, "Yep! There's **coordinating**, corre . . ." She stopped and tried to remember the long word. "Oh, yeah! **Correlative** . . ."

"And **subordinating**!" Chloe remembered.

Cailyn skipped ahead and said, "They sound hard but they're pretty easy!" Chloe ran to catch up and met Cailyn at the buffet. A hungry dog looked up at the table.

Chloe's eyes grew wide. "Look at all this food!"

Cailyn nodded, "Let's write down some of the food here. There's a lot. What kind of conjunction could we use to talk about a lot of food?"

Chloe took out her pen and said, "How about coordinating conjunctions? They join words or phrases together, right? Mr. Rosen says you can use the word **FANBOYS** to remember them."

Cailyn walked the length of the table. "That's right. Each letter in FANBOYS stands for a conjunction, so we can use *for, and, nor, but, or, yet,* or *so.* FANBOYS!"

Chloe looked at the delicious food. Then she scribbled in her notebook. "I know what we can write."

The buffet had deviled eggs <u>and</u> macaroni salad.

Cailyn said, "Let's add this."

People at the party can eat sandwiches with turkey <u>or</u> ham.

Chloe watched as more food was added. She kept writing. The dog tried to climb onto the table to get something to eat.

The food was for people, <u>yet</u> the dog kept trying to eat it!

Cailyn ate a huge brownie. "Then we could write this."

I was completely full, <u>for</u> I ate too much food.

Chloe and Cailyn started laughing.

Just then, they heard shouting. Cailyn and Chloe looked at each other. They each grabbed another brownie and ran to the volleyball net. Mrs. Carlson was playing. She saw the girls and waved. Cailyn got out her notebook.

"Okay," she said, scribbling on the paper. "Let's report on this game! We can use the next type of conjunctions: correlative."

Cailyn said, "Remember, correlative conjunctions are pairs of words. They stick together. If one is in the sentence, the other should be too." She put her arm around Chloe and squeezed. "Like you and me! Correlative conjunctions are best friends."

Chloe squeezed back. Then she flipped through her notebook. "Let's take a look at my notes from class. I wrote down the pairs of words. They are: either/or, neither/nor, not only/but also, and both/and. Does that sound right to you?"

Cailyn nodded. Suddenly, she ducked. A volleyball flew past her head. "This game is out of control!"

Chloe laughed and began to write.

The volleyball game at the block party was lots of fun <u>not only</u> for the players, <u>but also</u> for the spectators.

Cailyn grabbed Chloe's hand. They ran around to the other side of the net. There a little girl hopped from foot to foot. She yelled, "I want to play!" Her dad answered back, "In just a minute!" Tears started to well up in the little girl's eyes.

Cailyn took out her notebook and said to Chloe, "How about this?"

One little kid hoped to play volleyball. Either she would join the game, or she would cry.

Just then, a huge, bouncy beach ball took the place of the hard volleyball. The little girl joined the game. Chloe and Cailyn looked at each other in surprise. Chloe started writing.

Neither my friend nor I thought the adults would let the kids play, but both parents and kids can play with the big beach ball!

Cailyn put her hand up for a high five. "That's perfect, Chloe!"

A little boy ran below their raised arms. Cailyn heard him shout, "You're it!" She knew the kids were playing tag. She watched as kids weaved in and out of the chairs. They ran past the buffet table and the volleyball net and then circled back around.

Chloe said, "Ooh, a game! That should be super interesting for our article." Just as she said that, one of the kids fell down and hurt his knee. Cailyn and Chloe ran toward him to help. So did several adults. But the kid got up right away and kept playing.

Cailyn said, "I think subordinating conjunctions will be perfect for this story."

Chloe replied, "Great idea! I remember those! When you use a subordinating conjunction, you need to use another sentence to finish your thought."

"That's right!" Cailyn said. She flipped open her notebook. "And there are a bunch of these conjunctions: *after*, *because*, *although*, *before*, *unless*, *whenever*, *wherever*, *since*, and *now that*. Wow—that's just a start!"

Chloe asked, "How should we use one of them in a sentence?"

Cailyn was already thinking of an example. "How about this?" she asked.

Although the little boy fell, he kept playing tag.

Cailyn explained, "This sentence has two different thoughts in it: first, the little boy fell. Second, he kept playing the game. The subordinating conjunction makes the first thought incomplete. Imagine if I had written, 'Although the little boy fell' without adding anything else. You'd wonder what was next!"

Chloe looked over to the bouncy castle. "How about this for a sentence in our article?" she asked.

<u>After</u> the game of tag, the two reporters went into the bouncy castle!

Cailyn whooped, "Let's go!" Chloe and Cailyn ran to the bouncy castle. They dove in and began bouncing up and down. Sometimes they bounced right into each other. They couldn't stop laughing.

Cailyn bounced up and down, "*Because* I'm laughing so hard, my stomach hurts!"

Chloe bounced right into her and the two fell down, holding their stomachs from laughing. "*Whenever* I'm with you, my stomach hurts from laughing!"

Cailyn stopped suddenly. "Hey! We're using subordinating conjunctions!"

Chloe stopped, too. "I guess they are pretty easy, after all! We should go finish our article, don't you think? Want to go to your house?"

Cailyn nodded and the two girls slid out of the bouncy castle. They ran over to Cailyn's house, which was only one house away.

Once inside, the girls sat at the kitchen table. Cailyn said, "I have a great idea to end the article. Let's come up with a couple of sentences that use all three types of conjunctions!"

Chloe closed her eyes and thought for a minute. Then she perked up. "I know! Let's start it like this."

Although the buffet and the bouncy castle were very fun, the best part of the block party was seeing our neighbors!

Cailyn bounced in her seat. "Here's another one."

Both the reporters of this story and the whole block had a fun time.

"What do you think?" Cailyn asked. "You used subordinating and coordinating in your sentence, and I used correlative."

Chloe smiled. "We did an awesome job, so I think we will definitely win that prize for the best article!"

Know Your Conjunctions

Conjunctions connect and combine words in sentences. Not every sentence needs a conjunction. However, they can help you pack your sentences with more information. Imagine you are describing food on a table. You could use many sentences: There are noodles. There are meatballs. There are drinks. Conjunctions can help you combine these: There are noodles, meatballs, *and* drinks. *And* is an example of a coordinating conjunction.

Correlative conjunctions are different. They work in pairs to talk about different options: *Either* he will drink milk, *or* he will drink water.

A third type is the subordinating conjunction. Subordinating conjunctions help you add more information, such as a reason for something: *Because* he was hungry, he ate all the meatballs. They can also say when things happened: *After* dinner, she drank a milk shake.

Page 8 talks about FANBOYS, a word you can use to remember several different coordinating conjunctions. They are *for, and, nor, but, or, yet,* and *so.* Try to find examples of all of these conjunctions within the story!

Writing Activity

Conjunctions are helpful when you want to squeeze more information into fewer sentences. Try writing a short story that uses lots of conjunctions. Use coordinating, correlative, and subordinating conjunctions. Then, rewrite the same story without using conjunctions at all.

How did the story change? Did removing the conjunctions make the story longer? Did it get easier or harder to read? If you found these two stories in a book, which would you rather read?

Glossary

conjunctions: words or sets of words that help connect and combine words and sentences.

coordinating: a conjunction that joins together words, phrases, or sentences.

correlative: a conjunction that is a pair of words that joins different parts of a sentence.

FANBOYS: a handy way to remember seven coordinating conjunctions: *for, and, nor, but, or, yet, so.*

subordinating: a conjunction that often starts a sentence but can't stand on its own. Another thought is needed to complete the sentence.

For More Information

Books

Cleary, Brian P. Illus. Brian Gable. *But and For, Yet and Nor.* Minneapolis, MN: Millbrook Press, 2010.

Loewen, Nancy. Illus. Sara Gray. *If You Were a Conjunction.* Minneapolis, MN: Picture Window Books, 2007.

Walton, Rick. Illus. Mike Gordon and Carl Gordon. *Just Me and 6,000 Rats.* Layton, UT: Gibbs Smith, 2011.

Websites

Conjunction Game: Turtle Diary
http://www.turtlediary.com/grade-1-games/ela-games/conjunction.html
This game will help you practice picking the right conjunctions.

Conjunction List
http://www.towson.edu/ows/conjunctions.htm
This website has a helpful chart listing lots of conjunctions.

About the Author

Megan Atwood is a freelance writer and editor in Minneapolis, MN. She has two cats. Their names are Albie and Genevieve.